FROM HUMBLE BEGINNINGS TO REALIZING A DREAM

FROM HUMBLE BEGINNINGS TO REALIZING A DREAM

LETSHEGO TAU

PARTRIDGE
A Penguin Random House Company

To order additional copies of this book, contact
Toll Free 0800 990 914 (South Africa)
+44 20 3014 3997 (outside South Africa)
orders.africa@partridgepublishing.com

www.partridgepublishing.com/africa

Acknowledgements

This book is dedicated to all those who believe and work hard to chase and live their dreams. You may use it as a guide for motivation.

Writing this book has been a tough journey, at the same time an enjoyable experience that I can't compare to anything. I guess it's true when they say following your passion is greater than following everything that presents itself to you.

A special dedication goes to my wife Mpho Tau and our beautiful children Omolemo, Reitumetse, and Remoneilwe for enduring all the suffering and all the sacrifice I had to make while I was working late nights, weekends, and most of the time, not being able to see to your well-being. You are the reason for the birth of this book.

To my mother Elizabeth 'Ouma' Tau, who gave birth to me, loved me, and raised me in the absence of a father figure. You are a star, Olady; you are the reason why I am where I am today. Much love.

To my dear brother Itumeleng McDonald Tau, who motivated me as a young boy to be more like him, thank you for being there for me and the friendship we have.

Another special thanks goes to my two pillars of strength when I was at varsity, and they are Aunt Puleng 'Ampu' Mara and Aunt Ntswaki Nene.

To my pastor Pa Tubane from New Life Church, who always inspires me to write every Sunday through his ministry that is always full of motivation, you are the best, Pa.

A special shout-out goes to each and everyone who will be getting a copy of this book, you guys rock big time. I will produce more inspirational books until my last breath.

To God be the glory, he is the reason for existence of this manuscript. Thank you, Father.

My Story

The year was 1984 when I was born; I remember growing up in a family that depended on a single parent (mother) who made sure that the absence of a father was never felt by either me or my brother. This woman worked as a cashier for the clothing store known as Smart Centre and later at a furniture store called Lewis furniture shop in small town called Wepener situated in the Free State province (South Africa). This powerful woman always made sure that there was food on the table each and every day for her family. I would hear other kids saying that they went to bed with an empty stomach but I'm glad that my brother and I never experienced that; we never went to bed with empty stomachs, not once, not ever.

We lived in a two-roomed house with a shack at the backyard, which we used as our bedroom and most of the time as our chilling spot where we would enjoy listening to music. We were not only dependent on our mother's salary for survival, but also sold African beer (which is a beer made out of brown bread, yeast, pineapple, sugar, and tap water in a big container).

It's funny when I think about this ordeal now, since back then when you came from a background where you were selling African beer at your home, your schoolmates would make fun of you that you smelled of the African beer and they were sure that you sometimes drank that African beer and they would laugh the hell out of you.

At the time I would also feel ashamed about my background, and unfortunately had nothing to do about it, but I always had a feeling that I would not end where I was at the time (I always believed my then family situation was preparing me for great things to come).

What motivated me a lot in helping my mother selling the African beer was that she would make a point that every year in December when other kids would make a trip to Bloemfontein City (the capital city of the Free State province in South Africa), to buy clothes for Christmas, my brother and I would be spoilt to the core and would even look better than those children who had both mothers and father figures in their lives with good jobs.

Let me take you through the journey of my life:

It was 2001 when I completed my grade 12 at Qibing Senior School in Wepener. What I enjoy the most is that I had a chance or an opportunity to further my studies after completing my high school years.

It's really humbling to know that the woman (my mom) who played the role of both mother and father in my life made sure that she set aside all her savings from her salary which was then at an average of R3,000 a month from the furniture store she worked for and from the African beer which we sold at home by then.

I believe whoever that said 'real life begins after school' knew exactly what he/she was saying. One would take note of children who came from better backgrounds and they had all the nice things in the world the poor could ever dream of during school days but that entire achievement seemed to be short-lived, and believe me, it meant nothing when the life after school began.

After completing my grade 12, I realized that other parents did not do justice to their children and they would ensure their children would wear expensive clothes and have all the best things at the time, but ultimately forgot that children must study further after completing their highest studies at the end of their high school completion.

I realized that I was one of those fortunate children to have a parent that compromised much for her children and devoted her life to seeing her children succeeding in life, by ensuring better education at all times for her children.

This woman compromised a lot to see me and my brother becoming successful in life.

With the character displayed by my mother for our survival, I learned that it doesn't necessarily take a recognized profession to provide for your children, as my mother did not possess any educational recognition but worked hard instead.

All that it took her was to believe in me and my brother and give us a chance to further our studies. I'm glad we did not disappoint her as we both graduated from two highly recognized and respected universities in the country (South Africa) with high educational qualifications.

In 2004, my life at university level then began.

They say moving from a comfort zone to the world of the unknowns is a very scary feeling that no child can easily adjust to. I remember leaving home in the beginning of the year 2002, coming to Bloemfontein, where I was accepted at one of the universities to further my studies. It was not easy at first but I adjusted to the life of the city.

I had no idea on what career choices I needed to choose from when I was in my last year at school; thanks to the help of my aunt who advised me, I chose public management as the career of choice.

During my time at varsity, I realized that if you don't know what you want in life and why you chose to further your studies, distractions will always be part of your life, and believe me, you will never get anywhere. Some students deceived their parents that they were studying and doing well, only to find out that they were living expensive lives at their flat apartments which were paid with borrowed money from their parents for their own good, and never realized the importance of being afforded the opportunity to study, by their parents.

A wise man once said if you are on the journey and you are not sure where you are going, anyone that you meet on the way can easily make you follow their dreams and you might end up not reaching your own.

I met different kinds of friends at university, those that thought my background was better than theirs and intended to use me for their benefit (financial support). I met girlfriends who would not stand any rainy times and would just dump you for a better boyfriend that drove a nice car and had a nicer apartment than yours.

Life in the university was never easy for me, as I had to focus on my studies and try to ignore all the glitz and glamour the university life brought. I remember some of my classmates who would easily end their educational careers with alcohol abuse and taking drugs. I must say, coming from the background where I came from assisted me in making it in the university.

By 2004, I finished my studies, and by 2005, I graduated from the same university for my national diploma in public management, which was and still is a great achievement.

Today, I stand proud and believe that a journey of where I came from made me realize there was more to be achieved out there.

I hope this book will touch you and make you realize there is a potential and you should never think small of yourself. Always know that your current situation will never be your future reality only if you want to change it for the better.

May you enjoy every chapter of this book as it is written to inspire and transform you into someone you never thought you could ever be.

Enjoy!

Choices We Make in Life

In 2005, I had a dream to study further and obtain a qualification of bachelor's degree in public management, but life situations would not allow me to study further and I had to look for a job.

My mother, who had been supportive to me in the last three years of my studies, lost her job, and life then started to be a bit difficult for both myself and my brother. All thanks to my two aunties (Aunty Ntswaki and Puleng) who were so helpful and offered me a helping hand financially until I managed to find myself; may God bless them more.

We all know that the choices we make in life either take us to the positive or negative side of life. I was so fortunate that I managed to get a job in one of the clothing stores in Bloemfontein when I couldn't study further; for me, it was an achievement since I had no means to survive and take care of myself after completing my three-year diploma.

I worked for a period of two years (from 2005 until early 2007) for the same company and encountered some distractions in between. I have realized that sometimes we live life to impress others at our own expense and end up not going anywhere in life.

The job position I had at the time was a cashier and a sales representative for the company. I earned enough money to live within my means at the time but chose to live beyond my means and that was the beginning of troubles in my life. I chose to live in a flat in town and I could not manage the lifestyle I chose, but you know in life we sometimes set unreasonable goals, not knowing where they will take us. Unfortunately, I happened to lose my job at the clothing store I worked for, over the life of impressing friends and girlfriends and things just got out of control and the hardships of life began.

All friends who used to visit, sleep over at my bachelor flat vanished and I never heard from them ever again; that's when I realized that in life if you don't know where you are going, others will make you help them arrive at their destinations and you will never realise your goals until such time you change your mindset and grow from the mistakes you've made in life.

I moved out of the flat I used to live in and had to hit the road to living in the township area, where the rent was lower and the living standards were much lower than those I lived around before. The good life I lived while I was staying in the flats just vanished, and I had to adjust my life to that of the lower class; I had no choice at all.

In the midst of all the highs and lows life threw at me, I was fortunate to have my two aunties' support, and they both saved me from going home (Wepener). They did what they could for my survival while I was looking for another job. I never went to bed with an empty stomach; they provided rental money, food for me to survive.

Fortunately in a period of a month after losing my job, I applied for a job related to my qualifications in the government sector and I was hired by Free State Provincial Treasury, where I trained as an intern in the internship programme designed to cater to graduates who finished their studies and could not find a job, and I never looked back, and worked hard to prove to myself that I could become someone better.

The thought of losing my first job became an inspiration and a tool to focus my attention more on becoming responsible for my life.

In 2008, I was promoted to the department of health, where I managed to obtain my bachelor degree in public management which had been a long-term goal I wished I could reach, and that was a big achievement for me since I was the second at home after my aunt to have obtained a degree.

Fact about life

What you throw at *life* is what *life* will throw back at you.

Lost and Finally Finding Yourself

I remember when I started working at Free State Department of Health in the beginning of 2008; it was a feeling that I have ever wanted all of my life, to be independent and making money out of a career choice I had made.

In my mind, I thought having a stable job with a stable pay cheque every month meant that you would always have money every day of the month, but it was the beginning of real-life experience. I found myself earning R7,000 a month after deduction, and let me tell you I felt like I could buy everything in the world and still have my bank account smiling at me. Surprisingly it wasn't how real life was.

It would only take me half a month until I would have nothing in my bank account, and making ends meet before the end of the month would be Mount Everest to climb. I lived in a four-roomed rented house and only had one thing I bought from my salary to be proud of, which was only a music system (a Sony DVD player); the rest was a disaster.

I must say, when you don't have a plan in life, you will find yourself living beyond your means and have no direction of where you are going. In most situations, you find a lot of people working for big companies and earning good money at their jobs, but having nothing to show off that they earn better wages. I want to warn you to be careful of overcommitting yourself, living the life of unnecessary debts and impressing people who don't even care about you.

I learned later in life that there are good and bad debts, and what is important is to equip yourself with the right knowledge of how to use money efficiently. A lot of people say they want to earn as much money as they can, but have forgotten about the principle of learning how to save and use the little money they have efficiently.

I would hear my aunt emphasizing the principle of saving money, but to me it would always sound like a new song every time she drilled that thought in my mind.

I must admit that for most guys walking down there in the streets looking good, living in nice places, driving nice cars, and looking well taken care of, there is always the presence of a real girlfriend or real woman behind that man.

I have seen it with my eyes that living the way I was, was never going to take me anywhere in life, thanks to my then girlfriend and now my wife (Mpho Tau) for seeing that I was struggling financially and making efforts in helping me with my spending habits (I believe true love still exists out there).

It doesn't take a rocket scientist to figure out that most academics may do well in their studies while at universities or colleges, but may not have any idea when it comes to managing money and using it wisely.

We all want to live better lives, I know, and please don't get me wrong if I say there is no point in waking up early every day going to a job where you find yourself paying other people first and putting yourself last.

In my opinion, it's only a small number of people that truly find themselves after being enslaved by bad debts and recovering; I may not know your current financial situation but I hope this chapter has touched and given you a different approach about life in general.

Let my bad financial experiences be a valuable lesson for you to find yourself in making well-informed decisions about your life and, most importantly, your family.

Fake and True Friends

Some friends are true friends indeed; some are just part of your life and soon you will not even remember what their purpose was in your life, hate or love, it's true.

I have met a lot of friends from the beginning of my life journey, at university, and I'm still meeting them every day of my life. What I have realized is that there is always something that I would always pick up in every friendship I make. I would ask myself questions such as, What impact are these people having on my life? Are they draining me or empowering me?

I think you will agree with me if I say there are those friends who befriend you because of things that they think you may bring to them. There are those that get attracted to you because of your sense of humour and really enjoy your company. There are those whom you learn a lot from and add value to your life. Lastly, there are those who pretend to be true friends to you but they are your worst enemies.

It is OK to have a friend or friends in a space where you spend most of our time, but it is also important to know what boundaries and limits you need to set for yourselves when involved in any friendship, as you may somehow expose yourself to people who pretend to be friends and they are just not.

A friend of mine once told me a story of him wanting to start a taxi business service as additional income on top of his salary. He told me that one day while he was at work, he and his two colleagues/friends were having a tea break and sitting in a tea room having a conversation on how can they improve their lives, particularly their means of survival (income).

He said an idea came to his mind about starting a taxi business venture. He thought about the idea for some time until he made a decision to approach a bank that could lend him some money to kick-start his business idea. Fortunately, the bank let him borrow money to buy a vehicle which he used as a taxi for operation of his business.

He shared all the good news with his colleagues/friends, and they looked excited and congratulated him on the idea he came up with. It wasn't that long since he had bought the vehicle for the business idea he had, the same vehicle was stolen within four days after he had bought it, and his dream was shattered.

What's funny about his story is that his vehicle had passed all vehicle tests before, on the day it was stolen, and was ready for operation the next day. Remember this guy shared all the good news with his friends at work before; he was so open to them and thought they were real friends.

Up until today, he is still in the dark about who stole his car as he was always sharing his dreams with his two best friends.

The point I'm trying to make in this book about this guy's sad story is that we may feel comfort in the friends we make, but not all of them wish us the best in life or want us to succeed.

Be careful with whom you share sensitive information and your goals; in most times, jealousy makes other people do evil things to those who think they have true friends.

I still believe true friends still exist out there but they are hard to find; fake friends are always there and are a group of good pretenders who suffer from the syndrome called Pull Him Down (PHD).

Always keep your eyes open, and good luck in making real and true friends.

To Succeed or Fail: It's a Choice We Make

In life, some are born with a silver spoon in their mouth, some are born from the middle-class families, and unfortunately there are those who wish they could have been given a chance to choose backgrounds. The reality is, we have no choice in choosing families.

Ask yourself, if we were afforded a chance to choose our parents, we would all choose to be born in rich families with rich parents so that we could all get what we want when we want it.

I really believe that everything happens for a reason.

We all deserve a chance in life; and for every successful family out there, they were all afforded a chance and they grabbed it with two hands; that's why today they are successful.

When I was growing up, I used to think that coming from poor background meant you would remain there until the day you die, only to realize later that we all have choices to change our bad realities into better ones.

I remember there was a boy my age (ten years of age at the time) who was my neighbour; this boy was very good with numbers. My mother used to make us compete with each other as a form of giving us motivation to work hard at school. She would promise both of us that should anyone of us manage to get the numbers right, she would buy the winner anything of his choice as a reward.

I wish you could see how this boy would beat the hell out of me with numbers. I even sometimes felt like he was going to be adopted by my mother as one of her children as I watched how much my mother believed in him and would always tell us how dedicated this boy is; you would hate him for a moment.

The challenge with this friend of mine was that in his family, no one had any idea that he was the whiz-kid of numbers.

Unfortunately this guy did not have enough motivation to keep him positive and focused in life, and he ended up giving up on his dreams. He dropped his studies when he was in grade 8 and mixed with wrong friends; his life turned out to be difficult even more and his dreams were all over.

I met him recently, and it's sad to see him struggling to make ends meet. He once said to me he wished he had kept focus and worked hard; maybe he would have been somebody today.

A wise man once said, strike the iron while it's still hot.

My advice to you out there is, never allow distractions of life to take over your dreams; you are bigger than those distractions. Keep focus and one day is one day.

Giving Back

Life is somehow fascinating when you look at it; we all started as children learning all that we could when we were young.

We learned to brush our teeth and bathe ourselves through the guidance of our parents, and eventually we grew up until our inputs in decision making in our families matters every step of the way. By that I mean we become mature and add value to our families and are then regarded as responsible adults.

Most of all, we happen to be in control of our lives and those that are close to our hearts.

There is something I'm trying to bring your attention to, and that is extending the helping hands and not just limiting them only to those close to ourselves.

There is an old friend of mine by the name of Itumeleng, whom I attended a primary school with, when I was in standard 4 in the primary level.

This guy had passion for physical science and mathematics. I remember one year when we attended a winter school programme presented to all interested grade 12 learners at

Central University of Technology Free State, this guy was vocal in most classes we attended.

I am sure all the other students who did not know him very well were always bored by his character of participating on every question asked in most lectures when we attended the winter school. In South Africa, we refer to those people as Mr/Mrs Know-it-all (Tsibinki in South African vernacular).

What we did not foresee was what this guy was all about; he paved his life for himself and was also learning all that he could to become someone great one day.

Today this gentleman is an engineer in one of the respected mines in Mpumalanga, South Africa. The courage of working hard took him to great heights.

I often meet him during December month back home (Wepener) during Christmas holidays. What surprised me about this young man is that he is successful and doing well in his career, and most of all, he is investing most of his money for the future years to come.

I sometimes wished I was him.

When it comes to caring about other people and making a difference in their lives, this young man is amazing. Recently he took one of his best friends he grew up with, applied for him a job in the mine he is working for, and through God's mercy, that friend of his was hired for the job.

The point I am trying to make about this man is, he does not forget where he come from. He tries everything in his power to plough back to the community he comes from. I heard that every year when he is home he takes some of his old friends who are unemployed back to his working place and ensures supporting them until they get jobs and change their lives for the better.

In my opinion, a character shown by this young man is the character of the leader; he does not only think for himself and doesn't want to be recognized alone. He thinks and cares about others.

In South Africa the spirit of ubuntu (togetherness) does exist, but in most cases, people are selfish and believe all great things must come their way only and not for others. I have seen situations where one person may be holding a powerful position in an organization and that same person will be hiring his/her family members only, no matter how unqualified they may be.

I truly think if we could all think like Itumeleng, we could all make an impact to all those less fortunate people in our communities so that we can help them get somewhere in life.

I always believe we are where we are because of someone or a group of people who believed in us. We may be qualified in terms of qualifications for the jobs we are doing, but if no one believed in you, you wouldn't be where you are.

Help someone less fortunate out there; trust me, you will never believe the blessings God will bring to your life. I believe for most of us to get ahead in life, we need to start to change how we think about each other.

Africa is a beautiful continent that is full of opportunities that we as Africans need to take and share with one another to take it where we want it to be one day.

My biggest dream is to see people helping each other to get ahead in life, not people who look down on others.

There is a saying that I like, and it goes like 'Together we stand, divided we fall.' The choice is yours.

Running Your Own Race

In everything we do in life, we need motivation, hard work, and most of all, dedication in order to reach our set goals. I have learned that the best possible way to test how capable you are in achieving something great is to have something to motivate yourself first.

In the beginning of each year, a lot of people set their goals and refer to them as their New Year's resolutions; the problem with that is when all these goals are set, people copy each other. Some of the people don't really understand the importance of setting goals and working hard to reaching them.

Being motivated is a nice feeling, but it does not only end there. Motivation is just not strong enough to assist you to reach your goals; you may be motivated to work hard in achieving something in your life, but if you don't work hard to achieve it, I guarantee you that you will never in your lifetime reach your dreams.

They say hard work helps you reach your goals; to dream and think things will bring themselves to you is just not good enough. Don't get me wrong; it's normal to dream about what we want to reach in life but we must work hard to reach such goals.

I have listened to interviews of most sportsmen around the world; a lot of them emphasize only one thing. That is the principle of running your own race in whatever you do.

I once watched one of the greatest runners in the world, by the name of Usain Bolt, in his motivational video; he emphasized that when you want to be great in what you are doing, the only competition is yourself. Always strive to beat yourself in everything you do. Improve on yourself.

By that, he meant that he focuses his energy on becoming someone better in what he does, not what others want him to be. He is running his own race rather than running other people's races.

Focusing on yourself will help you to learn a lot about who you are; you are able to learn your weaknesses and strengths.

A lot of us always stress ourselves out with 'What will other people say if I don't do this or that?' and the same people whom we stress ourselves about don't even give a damn about us.

We need to start loving ourselves so much and start spending more time on improving ourselves than on wasting our energies on things we cannot change, which are other persons.

It only takes you as a person and your attitude to change your situation in life.

Distractions and Money

There is an old saying that a man's greatest downfall is women he mixes with, alcohol abuse, and wrong friends. I don't know how true this is; I somehow think the statement is true though.

I have read a lot of books about successful guys who shared some of their valuable life experiences and their road from nothing to great heights. All that these authors have in common is the same message that you should at all times be aware of the pitfalls of life; most of them emphasize the power of association.

They say, 'With the power of association comes people who can either drain all your energies, or people who could bring something positive to you, it all depends on what people you want to attract in your life.'

I remember when I was still attending school, I used to have a very close friend that I was inseparable with, and in my opinion, that guy was one of the truest friends I have ever had in my life. When it came to schoolwork, I would learn a lot from this friend of mine who was a genius.

Unfortunately his father died when we were in grade 10 in high school and things started to get out of control; his life changed from good to the worst. He started having new friends when his father's pension fund paid out; it was all type of friends, the good versus the bad, and most of all, the worst ones were also part of the package. I don't want to talk about girlfriends; you can just imagine.

It is always a fact that with a bad friend, there will always be a lot of bad things associated. I tried to talk him round, but the stage was too big for him to ever take any advice from any one of his old friends. His schoolwork started deteriorating and that was a new chapter of his life.

He would go to parties most of the time and forgot about his schoolwork; the number of friends he had grew in a short space of time. He lived an expensive and fast life.

It did not take that long after his father's death, another death tragedy hit his home, and this time around, it hit him directly; he passed on at the tender age of sixteen. His future went down the drain just like that.

What I have learned from my friend's short life was that life gives no one any guarantee. For some people, they are fortunate to get a second chance and mend their ways, but for others, it is not always possible to see the second chance.

We need to take life seriously and live each day as if it's the last, but most of all, do the things we would never regret.

Never ever forget that when you have money you may find yourself associated with some people who are in your life for wrong reasons, so be careful who you associate yourself with.

Coins always make a sound but paper money is always silent. Keep yourself silent and humble.

Saying Goodbye to Our Dreams

Have you ever wondered why you are still where you are and don't see any changes in your life? The answer is always simple; you are where you are because of one thing, your mindset towards life.

If you decide to be negative towards everything that must be done and requires hard work from you, you will only produce nothing out of your laziness. Most people make me laugh sometimes; they say they deserve better than what they can produce, and that is totally insanity.

I have seen a lot of people in my work environment moaning and complaining that they deserve better, and all they produce is nothing. How can you claim what you have never worked hard for?

Most people believe that failure is a reflection of who they are, and what they don't know is, failure can change you to look at life differently; failure is the best ingredient of success, if you don't know. Take this for example: for a baby to be able to walk, he/she must fall a couple of times before mastering the tactics of walking.

Our school system sometimes fails us completely; you are taught not to ever fail in your grades and it's true that we all want to succeed all the time. But for most successful people, failure forms part of their successes, and they find and push themselves out of the failures they encounter.

They realize that they need to improve in what they are doing for them to become great in that.

I have heard of schoolchildren who would give up their dreams because they did not do well in their studies; some commit suicide, some give up school completely and fall into a trap of stealing for survival. I always recommend to a lot of negative people to focus their negative energies into positive energy and see what the outcome will be.

It's clear that the energy that you use to influence negative things, if turned positively, will produce positive outcomes. I always wonder why a lot of people would not use the same negative energy they possess and direct that same energy into things that may produce something positive.

Most people give up on themselves easily and don't want to go through trials and tribulations of life, and every time things go wrong on them, they easily blame others for their own mistakes.

In South Africa, particularly in the poor communities, some people believe in witchcraft so much, and they normally claim that they are bewitched should any luck run out on anything they were once good at.

Saying goodbye to our dreams and aspirations is the easiest thing one can do, and it doesn't even require us to work hard in achieving that. All you have to do is to sleep all day and start blaming others for your misfortunes. It's up to you.

The following are best quotes extracted from forbes.com that will hopefully inspire you to look at failure differently:

1. Failure isn't fatal, but failure to change might be. – John Wooden
2. Everything you want is on the other side of fear. – Jack Canfield
3. Success is most often achieved by those who don't know that failure is inevitable. – Coco Chanel
4. Only those who dare to fail greatly can ever achieve greatly. – Robert F. Kennedy
5. The phoenix must burn to emerge. – Janet Fitch
6. If you're not prepared to be wrong, you'll never come up with anything original. – Ken Robinson
7. Giving up is the only sure way to fail. – Gena Showalter
8. If you don't try at anything, you can't fail . . . it takes backbone to lead the life you want. – Richard Yates
9. Failure should be our teacher, not our undertaker. Failure is delay, not defeat. It is a temporary detour, not a dead end. Failure is something we can avoid only by saying nothing, doing nothing, and being nothing. – Denis Waitley
10. When you take risks you learn that there will be times when you succeed and there will be times when you fail, and both are equally important. – Ellen DeGeneres
11. It's failure that gives you the proper perspective on success. - Ellen DeGeneres
12. There is no failure except in no longer trying. – Chris Bradford

13. I have not failed. I've just found 10,000 ways that won't work. – Thomas A. Edison
14. Success is not final, failure is not fatal: it is the courage to continue that counts. – Winston Churchill
15. There is only one thing that makes a dream impossible to achieve: the fear of failure. – Paulo Coelho
16. Pain is temporary. Quitting lasts forever. – Lance Armstrong
17. Success is stumbling from failure to failure with no loss of enthusiasm. – Winston Churchill
18. I'd rather be partly great than entirely useless. – Neal Shusterman
19. We are all failures—at least the best of us are. – J. M. Barrie
20. The only real mistake is the one from which we learn nothing. – Henry Ford
21. Failures are finger posts on the road to achievement. – C. S. Lewis
22. Winners are not afraid of losing. But losers are. Failure is part of the process of success. People who avoid failure also avoid success. – Robert T. Kiyosaki
23. Every adversity, every failure, every heartache carries with it the seed of an equal or greater benefit. – Napoleon Hill
24. You build on failure. You use it as a stepping stone. Close the door on the past. You don't try to forget the mistakes, but you don't dwell on it. You don't let it have any of your energy, or any of your time, or any of your space. – Johnny Cash

25. It's not how far you fall, but how high you bounce that counts. – Zig Ziglar

26. Failure is so important. We speak about success all the time. It is the ability to resist failure or use failure that often leads to greater success. I've met people who don't want to try for fear of failing. – J. K. Rowling

27. No human ever became interesting by not failing. The more you fail and recover and improve, the better you are as a person. Ever meet someone who's always had everything work out for them with zero struggle? They usually have the depth of a puddle. Or they don't exist. – Chris Hardwick

28. When we give ourselves permission to fail, we, at the same time, give ourselves permission to excel. – Eloise Ristad

29. With a hint of good judgment, to fear nothing, not failure or suffering or even death, indicates that you value life the most. You live to the extreme; you push limits; you spend your time building legacies. Those do not die. – Criss Jami

30. What is the point of being alive if you don't at least try to do something remarkable? – John Green

Going Big in Life

Some say start small, grow in what you do, and work even harder to make it big and achieve your goals.

I don't know what your feeling is on starting small; a lot of people happen to dream big and wish to achieve big things in life, but most of them end up living their fears instead of their dreams.

A long time ago, there was a boy who came from the farms to find better living conditions in a small town called Wepener; this young boy came from a poor family background and had to provide for his siblings and their grandmother as he was the eldest in the family.

He attended school during the morning, and after school, he would go and work for one of the local businessmen, known as Mr Paul, who ran a convenient store and lived not far from home.

What was different about this young man was the fact that he knew what he wanted in life and made sure his family struggle of the time never influenced his vision, instead serving as a motivation to work hard.

He studied and worked hard in school and also at the convenient store until he finished his school time. He was one of those unfortunate ones who never had the chance to study further after completing his high school studies. Financially he could not afford to further his studies.

What's inspiring about this young man was, he did not let his setbacks affect his life. He left his hometown to seek opportunities in a city.

On his arrival in the city, he lived with friends and family when he was looking for a job until he was hired as a taxi driver. He kept on working hard and saved money from the little salary he was earning until he managed to buy himself a taxi.

From entering a taxi business as the driver and owner, he worked his way up to starting a fruits and vegetables business where he hired some of his siblings to work for him in the city, which was a new chapter of his success story.

Some years later, after success of his small businesses, he was recruited to work as the sales representative for Land Rover South Africa in Bloemfontein, where he also did well and learned a lot about cars.

When most people would have thought this was the end of this young man's success, he then realized an opportunity brought by the South African government and took advantage of the government opportunities as a service provider for services and goods required by various government departments. He took full advantage of it and manoeuvred his way into starting a shuttle service and was awarded a couple of contracts by most of the government departments.

Today he owns a property in one of the expensive estates in Bloemfontein, called Woodlands; he owns and runs a car dealer outlet named after him, and most of all, he is forever humble and does not forget where he comes from.

He proved to his friends and people who never thought he could ever succeed in life that it's not always through formal education that you can be successful; self-knowledge can make you a fortune.

He came from humble beginnings to realizing his dreams.

Why It's Important to Follow Your Passion

A lot people live their lives pretending as if thcy never had anything they ever loved doing out of their hearts. This group of people often tells you that passion never pays bills; you need to focus on a steady income to make it in life.

I'm surprised every time when I look at successful people who never depended on anyone but themselves to realize their dreams to build their prosperous lives.

If you want to see the most influential, motivated, and passionate people in the world, look no further than those people in careers that require passion for success; you will be surprised.

Most of the world's greatest stars started out enjoying themselves in what they were doing and fell in love with it. Today what started out as a passion has become the extreme flow of income and lots of endorsements for those people.

I have seen ordinary people starting out as amateurs in their respective chosen careers, and ending up as professionals in what they are doing; all that it took for them was a dedicatcd heart, hard work, and the 'believe it will happen' attitude.

Most of the time, ordinary people often say ordinary statements about themselves and they are always happy with what life throws at them.

The following represent a secure mind who seeks security rather than opportunities:

- As long as I'm surviving, I am happy with my life.
- I must count my blessings; others wish to be like me.
- They would say, 'As long as I have my job . . .' They forget about downsizing that can happen at any given time.
- They always believe in security and never want to work hard to improve their skills or become better at what they do.

Passionate people always look out for opportunities in obstacles; they never run away from the challenges when they arise.

Most of the successful people come out of their shell when they are faced with challenges and prove to everyone that they are the best at what they do.

If you don't believe passion can pave the way for your success, look at tennis stars like Rafael Nadal, Roger Federer, and Novak Djokovic. These guys enjoy themselves in the court of play, and people pay a lot of money to see them playing tennis.

I believe when they started out, they never thought they could become who they are today, but they believed in following their hearts and building love for what they do, hence people don't mind paying a fortune to see these guys playing tennis.

For as long as you are not happy doing the job that you are doing, you will never find happiness in your heart. You will always read and follow scripts of others and be forced to watch others produce their own books and their life stories while you are just an ordinary spectator.

The following are some of the best quotes from influential people who followed their passion:

- Every great dream begins with a dreamer. Always remember, you have within you the strength, the patience, and the passion to reach for the stars to change the world. – Harriet Tubman
- There is no passion to be found playing small—in settling for a life that is less than the one you are capable of living. – Nelson Mandela
- Develop a passion for learning. If you do, you will never cease to grow. – Anthony J. D'Angelo
- Passion is energy. Feel the power that comes from focusing on what excites you. – Oprah Winfrey
- If passion drives you, let reason hold the reins. – Benjamin Franklin
- We must act out passion before we can feel it. – Jean-Paul Sartre
- It is obvious that we can no more explain a passion to a person who has never experienced it than we can explain light to the blind. – T. S. Eliot
- Nothing is as important as passion. No matter what you want to do with your life, be passionate. – Jon Bon Jovi
- You can't fake passion. – Barbara Corcoran

- You have to be burning with an idea, or a problem, or a wrong that you want to right. If you're not passionate enough from the start, you'll never stick it out. – Steve Jobs
- Yes, in all my research, the greatest leaders looked inward and were able to tell a good story with authenticity and passion. – Deepak Chopra
- If you feel like there's something out there that you're supposed to be doing, if you have a passion for it, then stop wishing and just do it. – Wanda Sykes
- If you don't love what you do, you won't do it with much conviction or passion. – Mia Hamm
- It is the soul's duty to be loyal to its own desires. It must abandon itself to its master passion. – Rebecca West

Turning Lemons into Lemonade

Every day of our lives carries a lot of challenge that we must overcome, and what is important is how we adjust to such challenges, come back strong, and become better people.

There are lots of stories that I have read about the people who have had bad situations and turned them around positively. One of the stories that touched me the most was the one of Oprah Winfrey, the world's most respected woman who grew up from a poor background.

This woman came from a family where she lacked close supervision and was exposed to several male relative and friends who sexually abused her, causing her to run away from her home on many occasions.

At the age of fourteen, she gave birth to a premature baby, who died shortly after birth. Her father was to provide her with the discipline that was lacking in her life.

She was informed that the only way she would change her life would be through taking education seriously, which she did. Oprah Winfrey became an honours student in high school; she was voted the most popular girl and joined her high school speech team.

She managed to have her own television show which is still highly successful and has also written six books and produced the film of the novel *Beloved*.

With the little said about this powerful woman, I believe there is a lot we can learn from her life experiences which started very badly and changed positively.

What this woman did was to turn lemons into lemonade; she has shown to the world that it's possible to turn your bad situations into better ones. Don't let life challenges determine where you are going. The poor background that Oprah came from did not determine her destiny, but made her realize who she was.

I'm always disturbed by people who allow other people to take advantage of them, being told they can't reach their dreams. The truth about life is, what other people think of you has got nothing to do with what you want to be in life.

Never in your life accept everything that life throws at you.

We live in the world where true friends are scarce to find; take time and ask yourself, who are those friends that add value to you and who are those that put a lot of strain on you and add no value to your life?

It's always difficult to know who could potentially leave a sour taste in your life; choose friends carefully. True friends never get angry or feel jealous when other friends prosper in life; they become inspired and feel proud.

Things the Rich do, the Poor Don't Do

There's a saying that goes like 'The rich will always be richer while the poor shall remain poorer.'

It's true that a rich mind will always think positive things, while the poor mind will always be lazy to think and always be discouraged most of the time.

It's a norm that successful people always have their days planned. Without writing our goals down, we will never attain any of our desired goals.

A study has shown that every day we have lots and lots of thoughts that cross our minds; what is important is for us to write some of those thoughts down.

A lot of rich people always encourage you that you need to look for an association of people who are rich in thinking; the truth is, with rich attitudes there is positive thinking.

People who have given up in life are normally associated with words such as 'I'm from a family of the poor, who am I to break the chain?' so be careful of the people you attract in your life.

The following are what the rich minds meditate on, most of their time:

- Good things are supposed to happen to me.
- In order for me to be comfortable, I need to be rich.
- They never say 'I'm broke'; rather, they use words such as 'I'm overcoming my cash flow challenges.'
- They always claim what they want.
- They believe the lack of money is the root of all evil.
- They know it's frustrating to be poor; no options are there.
- Having money assists you in getting control of your life, gives options, and allows you to live the life of contributions.
- They are willing to do things today others won't be doing in order to have the things tomorrow others won't have.
- They make discipline a major force in their life; an undisciplined life is an insane life.
- They make it OK to fail so that all things done wrongly will be in the state where they can be corrected.
- They believe you don't have to be great to get started, but you have to get started to be great.

It's Important to Spend Time with Yourself

We often feel bad and feel left out if our relations with other people are not in a good state, and we forget when things are like that, it is the right time for us to reflect back on ourselves.

I often hear a lot of people blaming other people if their own plans went bad. I don't know; maybe it's just how we are. I wonder if we have ever noticed that we spend a lot of time reflecting on what others are doing and forget about what we need to do.

Focusing your energies on other people makes you forget who you really are. You tend to think that all the great things are meant for those whom you always talk about and embrace a lot and think less of yourself.

I must say it's normal to have a personal mentor or a role model in our lives so that we can get motivated to achieve great things they have achieved.

I suggest you start spending time with yourself; the advantage of that is, you are able to reflect well on yourself and you can easily realize potential within yourself.

When you spend time with yourself, you become more focused on your life; things that looked small before, start to shape up because you now look at them differently.

It's not always through association with friends that you can enjoy yourself, but also, finding who you are and what your purpose is in life will help you to determine who you really are and where you are going.

If you don't know where you are going in life, someone is going to lead you and unfortunately you can never know if you are taking the right way until you arrive at his/her destination. Your dreams shall be just dreams and will never be realized.

The Power of Using Money

Money, power, and *respect* are powerful words and somehow influence the thinking of many people. Have you ever noticed people who are known to have lots of money, how they are treated?

Most are treated like little living gods and they are always respected because of the money they have. The point I'm trying to make is, don't be fooled by the amount of money others make or have; what is important is how these monies are invested and spent.

I have seen people who earn half a million or even above a million per annum but have money problems. The problem is, they live beyond their means and never expand their means, and their bills are forever expanding.

It's insane to overcommit your money and still expect to live a normal life; things will eventually catch up with you. People happen to copy other people without having any clue what it is that others are doing to sustain their expensive lifestyles.

Living life of impressing others will teach you a tough lesson, if you don't know. Never find yourself competing with your friends or neighbours because of what you imitate from them. Live your life on your own terms at your own pace.

I have had an experience of a friend who overcommitted himself with debts and could only come to work one week of the month and then he would be back on the day his salary would be paid.

The problem with this guy was, he committed his salary before it could even reach his bank. He would borrow from others and make promises that he would pay them at the end of the month and could not keep the promises he made.

His life was always miserable and you could easily read the stress he would have on the payday. His relations with most of his colleagues were compromised because of the borrowings he would make and end up not paying money back.

Another story that I would like to share with you is that of the middle-aged lady I happened to work with at one of the government departments. This remarkable lady taught me a lesson I will never ever forget in my life. She was a widow with three children and the only one as breadwinner.

What's inspiring about her is, she worked as a clerk who earned less than R50,000 per annum, but had the wisdom and knowledge to use money properly. I was surprised the first day I visited her at her house. She had built a big nice house for her family, and then furnished it with nice and expensive furniture.

You would think her children had support from both parents if you did not know; they attended reputable schools and were well mannered. It was amazing what I saw. The question I asked myself repeatedly was, how did she manage to be where she was with the little she was earning every month?

I reflected back on myself and wondered what inspired her to focus so much in life, as I felt earning more than what she earned, I was better than her.

Before I visited her home, I thought I was better than her, since I was her supervisor at work and earned better than her. The truth was that I did not have the knowledge of using money correctly, which was the difference between us.

I learned to never write off anyone because of positions they hold. I realized that it's not always about how much money you earned; it's more about how you spend it.

So I thought it would be useful for me—and hopefully for you too—to put together a list of some of the best quotes on wealth and money that I think will assist you:

- Before you speak, listen. Before you write, think. Before you spend, earn. Before you invest, investigate. Before you criticize, wait. Before you pray, forgive. Before you quit, try. Before you retire, save. Before you die, give. **– William A. Ward**
- It is not the man who has too little, but the man who craves more, that is poor. **– Seneca**
- Money is only a tool. It will take you wherever you wish, but it will not replace you as the driver. **– Ayn Rand**

- Not he who has much is rich, but he who gives much. – **Erich Fromm**
- Time is more valuable than money. You can get more money, but you cannot get more time. – **Jim Rohn**
- The person who doesn't know where his next dollar is coming from usually doesn't know where his last dollar went. – **Unknown**
- I don't pay good wages because I have a lot of money; I have a lot of money because I pay good wages. – **Robert Bosch**
- That man is richest whose pleasures are cheapest. – **Henry David Thoreau**
- Money is like love; it kills slowly and painfully the one who withholds it, and enlivens the other who turns it on his fellow man. – **Khalil Gibran**
- It's not the employer who pays the wages. Employers only handle the money. It's the customer who pays the wages. – **Henry Ford**
- Capital as such is not evil; it is its wrong use that is evil. Capital in some form or other will always be needed. – **Gandhi**
- When a fellow says it ain't the money but the principle of the thing, it's the money. – **Artemus Ward**
- He who loses money, loses much; He who loses a friend, loses much more; He who loses faith, loses all. – **Eleanor Roosevelt**
- Money is good for nothing unless you know the value of it by experience. – **P. T. Barnum**
- Happiness is not in the mere possession of money; it lies in the joy of achievement, in the thrill of creative effort. – **Franklin D. Roosevelt**

- Many people take no care of their money till they come nearly to the end of it, and others do just the same with their time. – **Johann Wolfgang von Goethe**

- Empty pockets never held anyone back. Only empty heads and empty hearts can do that. – **Norman Vincent Peale**

- If you want to know what a man is really like, take notice of how he acts when he loses money. – **Simone Weil**

- It's good to have money and the things that money can buy, but it's good, too, to check up once in a while and make sure that you haven't lost the things that money can't buy. – **George Lorimer**

- Money never made a man happy yet, nor will it. There is nothing in its nature to produce happiness. The more a man has, the more he wants. Instead of filling a vacuum, it makes one. – **Benjamin Franklin**

- You can only become truly accomplished at something you love. Don't make money your goal. Instead, pursue the things you love doing, and then do them so well that people can't take their eyes off you. – **Maya Angelou**

- Don't tell me where your priorities are. Show me where you spend your money and I'll tell you what they are. – **James W. Frick**

- Formal education will make you a living; self-education will make you a fortune. – **Jim Rohn**

- Buy when everyone else is selling and hold until everyone else is buying. That's not just a catchy slogan. It's the very essence of successful investing. – **J. Paul Getty**

- If money is your hope for independence you will never have it. The only real security that a man will have in this world is a reserve of knowledge, experience, and ability. – **Henry Ford**

Vulnerability vs. Love

I usually ask myself what is it that I can't cope with if the worst was to happen; the answer would be to deal with situations that I can't control.

I have a friend who has a child that suffers from cerebral disorder; this child is about six years old now and still going through various phases of therapy to assist her in her disorder.

What touches me the most is that both this friend of mine and his wife give this child unbelievable support and have tremendous love for her. I have never heard them complaining about the condition of this child.

Walking into their home, you are always surrounded by love, and they are real parents who teach their children good manners; they are an inspiration to me.

I have realized through them that we should never look at life challenges as negative but rather as a test that makes us better and assists us to look at life differently. Children need to be loved, and it's their democratic right to be cared for and raised in a good environment; it doesn't matter what birth conditions they may be born with.

One summer morning, I came from my usual training practice, and on my way to my house, I realized something strange about a guy who was walking past my gate. I came close to this guy, who seemed to be living on the street by expression of his look and the clothes he wore.

The strange thing about this guy was, he had no shoes on his feet; he was wearing socks, had torn pants and a jersey that looked very old and untidy. I greeted him and asked what size he was wearing.

The intention was to get his a pair of old shoes I was not wearing anymore. He greeted me back and looked scared at the same time. He thanked me for the offer I presented to him and insisted that he did not need shoes and was OK.

I realized that he had some form of mental instability and tried to beg him to wait for me so that I could get him a pair of shoes. He just kept on saying he was fine with socks on and did not need any shoes to wear; eventually I let him go and made my way to my house.

I was touched by this guy's condition and felt he was vulnerable and wondered where his family was.

From this experience, I felt that it is our duty when we have people with disabilities in our families, to take care of them. It doesn't matter how embarrassed they may make us feel; all that matters is, they have to be loved and taken care of.

It makes a difference to touch the lives of those less privileged and impact on them in a positive and special way.

Motivation to Do Something

Ever thought of how important it is to be healthy and eat right to keep up a good diet? Most of us live unhealthy lifestyles and expect our body systems to function well after all.

I have realized that most successful or rich people always find that little something to keep them focused and motivate themselves to do well in life.

In order for us to be able to keep focus on what we want in life, we need to find that special something that drives us from within.

For most people, waking up early in the morning every day and exercising is the best way to start their day. There's an old saying that goes like 'The early bird catches the worms.'

To keep focus requires a lot of motivation and determination. Without the two, one may be easily distracted and if distraction kicks in, motivation becomes just a word and loses its true meaning.

A lot of people tend to settle for less in life and find no motivation in what they have settled for. In my opinion, if you don't have any motivation in what you do, you will never come close to testing your potential.

Some of the successful people never thought they would be where they are until they decided to make things happen for themselves.

The advantage with creating things for yourself is, you end up creating products that you believe in and things become easier than trying to fit in what others have created.

I have realized that people with less or no motivation are good at defocusing others. They are good at creating stories that never existed and are also good storytellers and never do anything with what they preach.

There's a friend I have who thinks he knows everything about life; he would tell you about his other friends who hold high positions in the companies they work for around the world.

The question I always ask myself would be, since this guy sounds like he has right contacts all over the world, why can't he join his friends in high places? He is one of those referred to as trees that are judged by the fruits they talk about, not trees that are judged by fruits they bear.

There are those people who have already given up on life and don't see any potential within themselves; it's obvious they will never see any potential in others.

Living to Impress

A house in the hills and flashy cars are what most of us aspire to have in life, but I sometimes wonder what it is that these flashy items bring in return when they take money away from us.

Most of us, particularly boys, grow up knowing that the best toys we want our parents to buy for us must be a nice remote-control car, so that we can show it off to our friends every time when they visit us. What we forget is the feeling of showing off that starts at an early age, and our parents are the main contributors to that.

I don't say it's bad to buy children toys, but what we must remember is there are different types of toys available for children; some are just expensive toys with a purpose of playing and showing off only.

There are educational toys available in the market, and these toys may help our children in developing their way of thinking and becoming smart at the same time.

I remember when I was growing up, I loved cars and dreamed that one day I will get myself one and my dream will be fulfilled. One of the factors that pushed me so much was that my mom never owned a car and some of my friends' parents had cars at their homes and I would feel left out.

Life unfolded, and I grew up and managed to buy myself a car. What I didn't know was, cars carry a lot of costs to keep them running, and I bought mine with financing from the bank. I thought it would be an easy ride to pay the car monthly payment for the term I had agreed with the bank that financed me.

Things did not turn out the way I thought they would; I sometimes had to compromise, not eating out and buying myself nice clothes, as I had committed myself to a vehicle instalment that had to be honoured for a lengthy period of five years.

Some people see others driving nice cars and think life is as simple as it seems; they never know that these nice cars dig deep in their pockets.

Some people end up being blacklisted by financial institutions if they don't pay their monthly payments as per agreements entered into. Most people end up losing their nice cars and nice houses simply because of overcommitting themselves with bills.

I have seen people who live to impress going through some tough times because of wrong decisions they had made.

I have seen guys who make lots and lots of money from government departments as suppliers; these guys usually book VIP tables at expensive restaurants to the value R10,000 for impressing other people.

When these bookings are made, food and drinks are not included; they will be ordered separately.

I have heard a story of a guy who started from nothing and worked his way to the top. He saw an opportunity of doing business with government and was a beneficiary of Black Economic Empowerment, which was introduced by the South African government post-1994.

He excelled in what he was doing and made a fortune for himself. He used to drive nice cars and was always surrounded with nice women. You know they say the success of every man comes with a good woman, but with him it was the opposite.

He made lots of money with contracts secured with government departments he was contracted to; he partied like crazy and lived his life to the best to his best capacity.

The number-one thing he forgot was that the money and the nice life he had was never going to be there forever. He never made time to investigate what it was he could do with his money that would sustain him once his contracts with government departments had expired.

He never invested even a single cent from the millions he had made from his company.

Years and years passed by and he was on top of his game, he made headlines on local newspapers week in and week out. The media house happened to know him and he felt he had arrived.

It wasn't that long till he was declared bankrupt. We were all shocked to learn that his millions had just vanished like that; most of all, he had nothing to show as a form of an investment from the millions he once made.

I remember meeting him at some places I never thought a person of his character could be visiting. He started being a different person than what I read about him on newspapers when he was rich.

Life taught me a lesson that no matter what, we have to remember where we come from, in order to know where we are going. Living a life of impressing friends and other people leaves you empty.

We sometimes think our lives are determined by those close to us; some people become close to us for the wrong reasons and we are too blind to see that.

Again the power of association is very important; if you are a friend of a thief, you are most likely to become a thief too. Look at the people you associate with and take a moment and ask yourself if you see any future with them or not.

Life is not about what you can prove to other people. The best way to live your life is when you live it on your own terms, running your own race and focusing on your own plans.

A lesson learned from this once-a-millionaire story is, we never make time to be happy in our own personality, we always want others to appreciate us and forget to appreciate ourselves and accept who we truly are. Never live life to impress others; it's very dangerous.

Choosing a Family

It makes me laugh my lungs out when I think that we all came from families where we did not have a choice to decide what family we want to be part of, an option where we decide if we want to be part of the rich or the poor family we never had.

I think it's true when they say we live in the cold world; some people may judge others because of the situations they see them in or come from. I always observe that most people become disadvantaged because of their own backgrounds; most are judged based on where they come from and their surroundings.

When I was at university, I was living with friends and all of us came from different backgrounds; most of them had better families in terms of the financial well-being of their families.

There was a guy who used to have money almost every day of the month; he lived a good life. Whenever he wanted to eat anything, it was always possible for him and we would always wish to be like him.

You know when there are conversations about telling others what background you came from, it was always embarrassing to engage in such topics, nothing interesting I could refer to about my background.

I guess it's important to be proud of where we come from as there are lots of experiences that we must be happy about.

It was even worse to know that even ladies would not dare to bother looking at me at varsity as they were also looking for those guys who had money to support them financially.

I've had a situation where there was a beautiful girl I admired at the time; I remember approaching her with the intention of making her my girlfriend. She told me that unfortunately I did not meet her requirements of an ideal guy she had in mind. She made me aware that I could not afford her based on what she could see in my dressing style and my lifestyle in general.

I guess she had a point even if I was hurt by her honest remarks. It was painful to me that my background represented who I was at the time without even mentioning it to her.

But what most people forget is that our poor backgrounds have got nothing to do with what the future holds for us. What always surprises me is, most people live for the moment and forget that there is always the next day and it might be better than today.

Back at varsity, there were those guys who came from the same or similar environment I came from, and the problem was they wanted to impress the rich students that they could also afford the lifestyle the rich were living at varsity. You would see them on weekends buying expensive drinks and impressing girls. They would forget that the rich guys were just a phone call away from getting more money from their rich parents to replace the splashed money.

As for these guys, they would come back and ask for loans from other students to at least be able to have something on the table while they waited for the month to end.

Most of them did not finish their studies because of the associates they would have and changed courses year in and year out.

What I came to realize was, we should never write anyone off in life, because what they are today has got nothing to do with what they will become in the future.

It's all in the mindset

I guess we are born this way; by that I mean we are born the way we are. Some are born with multiple talents, some must work really hard to realize their hidden potential, and most never achieve anything in life; that's the nature of life.

Some people are so fortunate to live to tell that they were born with silver spoons in their mouths; for most, that feeling will remain a mystery in their lives.

I don't know if it's true that with money comes power and respect, or it's just what people think.

I have read a book that classifies different groups that are there, and these groups shall always be there as life is never easy for everyone to fall into one group.

These groups are classified as

- The poor
- The middle class (average people)
- The rich

The difference between these groups is, each one of them thinks differently about the other.

Those classified as poor always sideline themselves from other groups and feel good to be called 'ooh, shames of this world'. Be careful how you classify yourself.

Being poor does not necessarily mean coming from a poor background; having a poor context and little efforts to learning and empowering ourselves may easy contribute in making us poor. A lot of people think poor people come from a generation of poor families, but don't realize that how we look at life empowers us to become great, ordinary, or poor.

Ask yourself, how many ordinary people and poor people do you know in your surroundings? It's almost everyone that you know, but rich people are few, if not any around you.

Sometimes a poor context can make you so dumb that you don't see any opportunity when they present themselves to you. A poor mind thinks an opportunity may come wrapped in box and present itself.

The reality is, a clear mind is able to see things a blurred mind can never ever see and takes advantage of it.

The way we think determines how we want to reach our goals and the things we are willing to do to achieve what we want to achieve.

This is how the poor mind thinks:

- 'I am happy with the little I have', but the reality is, happiness comes with internal satisfaction, which most people don't ever live to achieve as they claim to be happy with the little they have.

- 'I cannot afford that'—they always limit themselves and never strive for anything challenging in their lives.
- They always look for easy outcomes and are at the back of everything and are good to judge when things go bad.
- They never want to learn anything new and are good in discouraging.
- They don't have ambitions and pretend to be happy when they are not.
- They always seek the easy way to do things, with little efforts to learn.
- They want to be recognized for doing nothing and can tell people how good you think you are when you don't promote them.
- They like to be felt pity for all the time.

With the mind like this, I can guarantee you nothing but a negative mindset which is going to contribute nothing but an unproductive and stagnant individual who will always blame others for his or her misfortunes.

The middle-class mindsets are those of individuals who make things happen for themselves and change their own realities into something tangible and productive.

What I admire the most about this group of individuals is, they take steps in what they believe can work for them even though sometimes fear seems to take advantage of them.

The rich mindset always takes action and learns through taking steps and is not fearful of the unknowns, and they possess the 'I can do it' attitude. They believe in building empires through tested systems or build their own systems and acquire people with the right skills, and they believe in sharing their fortunes with those less fortunate individuals. For an example, look at Patrice Motsepe.

I believe it takes a great mind to realize a lot about life; some minds allow life to throw whatever it throws at them and they are willing to accept it, no matter how small it may be.

It's a curse to believe you have no potential to become what God created you to be. Remember that in the Bible, Genesis 1: 28, God blessed man and his wife; and said to them, 'Be fruitful and multiply, and fill the earth, and subdue it; and rule over the fish of the sea and over the birds of the sky and over every living thing that moves on the earth.'

Remember there is always that small voice that tells you it's impossible, especially when things get tough.

Les Brown, one of the greatest authors, once said, 'Fear is false evidence appearing real.'

Ungrateful People

To wake up every day and live to see another day—it's really a blessing to all of us, and most people think it's a must-happen action, not a blessing at all.

I want to believe that we are always blessed to wake up every day and live to see each day.

Most of us sometimes don't appreciate a token brought before us which is called life, we decide to complain more about it and tell people how unfair life is and how bad luck we are if things don't go our way.

What we forget is, most of the successful people out there live to tell stories of how hard it was in the beginning for them to achieve what they have achieved and be where they are.

I once read an article where one journalist published a story about one of the greatest personalities in South Africa that I value so much; this great man is always bringing something positive to the less fortunate individuals, the one and only Mr Patrice Motsepe.

In the story published, it was alleged that Mr Motsepe was not giving back to the communities as he was proclaimed to be. I remember a public announcement he made about giving half of his money to charities across South Africa and Africa at large, and someone feels he is not doing enough. If I were that journalist, I would be ashamed of myself to even cover a negative story about an icon like Mr Motsepe.

The story covered a man who claimed that Mr Motsepe had neglected his birthplace and does nothing to bring positive change in the community where he was brought up and comes from. In my opinion, all positive efforts are always surrounded by negative people who will always have something to bring others down.

Most people depend on handouts so much that they will never do things for themselves to change their realities. They will always find excuses blaming others and do nothing to improve their own realities.

The challenge with most black South Africans is, they are exposed to too many opportunities and are too blind to take advantage of them. They always claim that the South African government is not doing enough, while they don't do a thing to empower themselves.

My Opinion on
Xenophobic Attacks

In South Africa, for instance, we have refugees who come to the country for asylum seeking, and these people decide to find means to sustain themselves and their families back in their homelands.

Most South Africans feel opportunities are taken right under their noses by the foreign nationals, but they don't realize that these people add value to them by running convenience stores close to them in the townships and also add value to those from whom they rent spaces to run their businesses.

I always wonder what is it that our angry South Africans are doing to maintain competition brought by the foreign nationals in this country. In my opinion, South Africans believe more in xenophobic attacks as a way of showing off how unhappy or frustrated they are with the government and foreign nationals in businesses.

I hate seeing foreign nationals being mistreated by our own brothers and sisters for the opportunities they decided to create that our own South African nationals do not even bother to learn so that they also become successful as well.

I don't turn a blind eye on those foreign nationals that run illegitimate businesses as there are those with bad business intentions in the country, where you find our sisters who turned to prostitution and are also made to depend on drugs to make money for their pimps who are mostly foreigners.

We sometimes forget that there are rules that every country passes in terms of foreign policies, especially those policies that govern business-related activities. In my opinion, foreign nationals who are in business add value to this country (South Africa), and I don't see any problem if they make money to sustain them and their families in the country of their birth.

Most South Africans are spoilt and they believe in doing nothing and blaming others for their own downfalls. If you could hear what other Africans say about South African nationals, you will be shocked they have learned that South Africans believe in shortcuts and don't want to get their hands dirty, but they always know where to point fingers.

I think when a person decides not to change his life for a good course, it's a bad choice made; they will always attract bad publicity and will never get ahead in life.

I have realized that life is what we make for ourselves, not what we expect others make for us.

Never be angry at others when they are ahead of us, rather find out how did they managed and always seek mentoring from those who are willing to assist you in becoming a better person in life.

There is time for everything in life and those who have patience and push themselves will know the truth of that statement. People need to appreciate the little done for them and our communities and must also think outside the box to become better in life so that we can realize opportunities before they even present.

Emotions Overcoming Patience

For most black Africans, life has never been that easy, especially if you came from rural or small places with lack of family support structure.

Most people decide to follow their passion and yet lack the drive to make it happen, but I've realized that it's harder for someone that does not have any strong family support base.

It's true that we need to be patient in whatever ventures we want to get ourselves involved in, and for some reasons, there are those people who live to never see their dreams coming true, because of not knowing which doors to knock on.

I came from a family in which I did not have the luxury of time to waste, and when opportunities were brought to my attention, I would grab them with both hands. For example, after finishing my matric, I was fortunate to be given a chance to go and study further at the university of choice.

What I did was to work hard and make sure that I present good grades every time when I went home for varsity recess vacation, and that made my mother proud and gave me a sense of knowing what I wanted in life.

Every time when I visited home, some of my friends would say it straight to my face that I would not complete the course I was studying at varsity; soon I would be home. They thought the little support from a single mother (my mother) was not sufficient to carry me until completion of my studies; they believed soon my mother wouldn't be able to support me financially and I would drop my studies the same year I went to varsity.

At varsity, there was also a lady who came from my home town and we lived in the same complex at the time. She would make fun of me every time I passed her room on my way to the library and would say to her friends that I resembled a bookworm, since I was studying every day.

She would somehow tell them in my presence that she understood the reason why I had to work hard towards my studies, as I lived in a two-roomed house and we were selling African beer back home for survival; to tell you the truth, I had no choice but to study very hard and change my family situation.

I believe the feeling of coming from a rich family was the only reason why she felt the way she did about me, as she looked at me as inferior to her.

At times I would be frustrated and become less motivated in studying hard, but I did not let emotions take control of me. I kept on and on and somehow became motivated by the negative remarks others would comment about me.

I told myself that the enemy outside would do no harm to me, and only I can build or destroy my life.

Years later, I completed my studies, I was fortunate to get find a good job and life started to pick up; to my surprise, I met my homegirl (the lady who stayed at the same complex with me who once told me that I was a bookworm). She looked surprised to see me better than I was before, and she could not contain herself and asked what my secret to success was.

She then asked me where I was working and if I could find her any job at the time. To my surprise when I asked her what she was doing for a living, she told me she worked for her mother and couldn't stand the little peanuts her mother was paying her every month and pleaded with me to find her a job where I was working.

I was shocked that she never completed her studies and went back home with nothing after the three years spent at the varsity.

I realized that one of her shortfalls she came across was the life of impressing others at the expense of her mother's wealth. Her mother only realized later that this lady only attended varsity for a one year and dropped her studies and could not complete her studies.

What life taught me was to never give up easily; some people are just in our lives to push us up to be great in life, but they will come in the form of negative people with negative remarks. They will always find means to bring us down but what they won't realize is, they will be some sort of courage to us and make us stronger and better people in the process.

Never allow your peers or friends take advantage of you and distract you from realizing your goals.

I believe some people are in the way and we should not get distracted by those who are in the way; we should just swerve and continue with our trips to the road of success.

Our Focuses

A lot of people would say, 'What would people say if I don't wear jeans with a designer label?' Some would also say, 'Does it really matter if my shoes are designer shoes?'

These are questions most people are faced with every day of our lives, and these questions have a powerful meaning within us.

It's always a great feeling to dream yourself out of a bad life situation that you may be faced with, especially if it's a tough one. In most times, people live to impress others and forget that these people whom they try to impress could possibly not be aware that their peers are trying to impress them and don't even care about the people trying to impress them.

I grew up with expensive taste in clothes and the reason for that was simple; my mother, who worked for a clothing store, would get 50 per cent off on all merchandise in the store, so she would buy us the best clothes the store could offer.

When I finished my matric and had to move to Bloemfontein to further my studies, I realized that a new life was about to start.

Most students from my home town who also had the chance to further their studies saved as much money as possible so that they could buy new clothes and look good in the universities of their choice.

In the year when I started my varsity studies, my mother had lost her job and I wished I could have turned back the time and had my mother working for the clothing store she once worked for so that I could buy the best designer labels with the 50 per cent discount she used to get. The reality was she was unemployed.

I would always wonder if girls ever looked at me when I was around the campus for my classes, because I would wear one pair of jeans three times in a week. It was not a matter of choice; I had only two jeans of inferior quality and I had no money to buy more clothing.

What I liked about the situation of the time was that through all challenges and peer pressure I encountered, I never lost any focus on the reasons why I was at the university. I would find peace in motivating myself by thinking of all people who would work hard in what they were doing and later reap rewards of their efforts.

My focus was so sharp that I was never distracted by any outside forces during my time at varsity. I always believed that one day things would work out the way I had wished.

I would meet friends who would prove a point that they came from rich families and had money but had no focus on things that matter the most, such as education.

Most people get easily distracted and defocused from what they want to achieve in their lives. We live the lives of others by interpreting exactly what others are doing. I believe we are all destined for greatness in life, but we need to be careful what we focus our minds on.

Eric Thomas once said, 'We focus so much energy on things that don't add value to our lives, and if we could take the same energy that we focus on negative things and turn it into positive energy, we will attract greatness in what we do.'

Other people view life as making a statement to others, and that is a problem.

A wise man once said when you walk into a house of a poor person content, you will be welcomed by a big TV set and state-of-the-art home theatre system, but when you walk into the house of the rich person content, you will find a library set up in one of the rooms in the house.

This means the more time you spend with yourself, the better you will become in learning more about yourself and your character. Reading is the best remedy for learning, and it eventually helps you to see life differently.

Most of us want to be appreciated all the time by other people and neglect ourselves so much that we feel less valued when we are not with others.

People who believe less in themselves always find well-defined excuses to blame others for the challenges they encounter in life.

To keep focus on everything requires some sort of motivation. I have never seen a successful person who is less motivated but successful at the same time.

Successful people focus on a good diet to keep their body as fit as possible; so is their mindset. They are not pushed around by the realities of life; they stand strong and always seek opportunities, calculate risks, and take action. They never settle for security, like ordinary people.

Most people want to be successful and never bother to work hard on anything that can make them successful. They always want to be pitied, and that's not how a successful life is approached.

Jack Canfield once said, 'Successful people maintain a positive focus in life no matter what is going on around them. They stay focused on their past successes rather than their past failures, and on the next action steps they need to take to get them closer to the fulfillment of their goals rather than all the other distractions that life presents to them.'

Why cry if people say they don't think your dreams are possible? They can't see what is in your mind, hence they think what their minds tell them is crazy. Never let anyone deter your dreams.

If you think your dream can happen, you are right and if you think it can't happen you are also right. A quote from Henry Ford

Is Money the Root of All Evil?

Some say money is the root of all evil, while others say how can money possibly be seen as the root of all evil? The lack and love of it should be seen as the root of all evil.

Most people wake up every day of their lives to go to jobs that they don't like; the main reason why they push themselves so hard is simply the lack and love of money, as well as seeking security.

These people are the ones that would always lead conversations of how the rich are so greedy and treat money as if it is their little god. Little do they know the secret of the rich: the rich know the importance of money, and they really take good control of the money they make.

It's sad how people with little knowledge of handling money think about money, and never make time to learn from the rich the importance of making money work for them.

You would hear poor people say it's better not to have money at all but to have peace. My question would always be how can you have peace when you are struggling financially and decided to work your whole life for the sake of making money?

A poor mind is always easy to influence and always agrees with everything that comes its way.

English translations of 1 Timothy 6: 10 vary, but they all say something along the lines of 'For the love of money is a root of all kinds of evil.' Notice the difference? It's about the love of money, not money itself, being the root of all kinds of evil, not all evil. A few small words make all the difference.

If any religion truly pointed out that money is the root of all evil, a lot of people would be trying to be as poor as possible. Money would be treated like a communicable disease. People would say, 'Please don't pay me so much; it's not right for you to spread money around.' Some people of faith do give away most of their income or take a vow of poverty so that they are better able to serve others and do good works, but most of those will describe their lifestyles as a special calling or a gift, something beyond what God requires of most adherents of their faith.

Even if you're not a believer, think about the logic of saying that money is the root of evil. If money were the root of all evil, only people who had money would do evil things, and the people with the most money would be the most evil of all. Though some people without money like to think that's true, it's not. Poor people can cheat and steal and assault and kill as well as rich people and people in between.

Looking at it from another angle, greed (the love of money) does cause people to do some pretty horrible things, but so do lust for power or sex, hatred, the desire for revenge, jealousy, and even some more noble things, such as a desire for purity or an attempt to protect someone else. Money is rarely on the mind of a man who drops a drug into a woman's drink so he can take her home practically unconscious.

I've sometimes heard 'Money is the root of all evil' used as an excuse for not saving, as if to say, 'I'm a better person if I'm poor.' But intentionally spending all your money as soon as you get it does not make you a better person (unless, maybe, you're giving it all away). Rather, it makes you irresponsible. On the other hand, making good use of your resources by saving for your future does not make you evil; it makes you more able to help others (or avoid needing the help of others) when the need arises.

It's your personal choice to think that money is the root of all evil or the lack of it that brings evil thinking. Good luck on the choice to finding out the real truth.

Push Yourself Beyond All Limits

I often hear lazy people saying when the going gets tough, just quit and sit and watch others; as long as you have the security you will be sorted.

Most people don't find anything to motivate themselves in life; they would rather decide to let go of their dreams when things get tough.

Most people live to never see their dreams coming true, simply because it's not easy to start something that requires hard work and devotion.

I have learned that for most people, the only thing stopping them from reaching their goals and dreams is the limits they set for themselves.

It's often when you meet your limits that you feel resistance, and things you want seem harder to achieve. Whether it is fear, doubt, physical abilities, or some other mental block, it can present a huge barrier to getting what you want.

Unfortunately, most people can't work past their limits and give up easily; the problem is they will leave their dreams unrealized.

In my personal experience, I have realized that it takes real courage to succeed in anything that requires hard work and time.

A few years ago, I decided to go to the gym and my intention was to keep a good weight and build on muscles. At first I made a lot of progress, but eventually I met resistance and my exercise goals became harder to attain.

I became complacent in my exercise routine by doing the same routine every day. I would wake up at five o'clock in the morning and run for an hour every day using the same route. It only took me a month till I started thinking that the routine was boring and gave up.

Looking back on it now, I can definitely see why I wasn't making any progress. Only after taking the kilometres I run every day into consideration and the time I would take, I started pushing myself to work harder and improve on every time made, to become better each time.

Most people believe that resources create success out of failures; I must say it is good to have required resources to perform well at what you want to succeed in, but nothing beats the will to succeed and the determination.

In order for us to succeed in what we want to achieve, we don't need anything but we need to be ready and willing to perform beyond our limits.

Dealing with a Loss

She used say to us, 'You must make sure that you take advantage of opportunities that come your way in life, because life is not easy and you will see it for yourself when you grow up.'

Those were the words my grandmother (Granny Mpho Mara) used to tell all her grandchildren; we would just laugh her off and think this old lady was just making fun and there was nothing serious about what she was saying.

The thought never crossed our minds that one day she would be gone and gone forever, and indeed she passed away in the year 2014.

Let me take you back to the years when I was growing up under the care of this great warrior (my grandmother).

I remember at age ten, I and my cousin (Dieketseng 'Keke') were in primary school, and both our mothers tried everything in their power to ensure that we got the best out of life; we would be under the care of our grandmother when both our parents were at work.

The old lady would really take care of us when were young, and she knew how to deal with the ill-disciplined children; my cousin can surely remember that.

We were so fortunate to have a grandmother like the one we had, she believed so much in children with good manners; had it happened that there were unmannerly ones, she would ensure that they became mannered.

This old lady was more like an open book; if she didn't like you as a person, she would tell you straight in your face and give you reasons why she felt that way felt about you. She never pretended.

She would emphasize the importance of her grandchildren getting education in any way possible and believed much in people who worked hard in life.

Losing her in 2014 was a tough experience to deal with and still is; she passed away at the age of seventy-six and had taught us a lot in life.

Many children are brought up by grandparents who, through thick and thin, ensure that they support them every step of the way.

It's sad when I think of children who treat their parents and grandparents badly. Some parents get killed by their own children over their old age grant they receive; we find out that the motive for that could be alcohol abuse and drugs.

I would read and hear news that most of these senior citizens are raped and brutally killed by lunatics who take advantage of their vulnerability.

I believe we all, at some time in our lives, lose close family members and friends through death. I suggest that we should celebrate the lives of the people we love while they are still alive than when they have passed on.

In my culture as a black person, there is this tendency of celebrating the lives of those who passed away by burying them expensively and trying to impress other people, while we forget that we should have celebrated their lives while they were alive.

Most people believe in giving the dead a decent funeral with all expensive services and making a statement to the mourners, but what they forget is life must still go on. All unnecessary costs incurred could have been saved for investments or savings for children.

Some children lose their parents at a very young age and are left with no option but to be under the care of their family members. What happens is some families mistreat these children and help themselves to the money left by the parents.

You would see expensive funerals in the black communities, and the same people forget that there is life that must still continue after burial of the lost loved ones.

In my opinion, it's insanity to prove a point to others by going expensive on funerals. It's wise to invest any money that may be left in the form of insurance than to spend it like there is no tomorrow.

I have realized that in the Western way, should they lose one of the family members, they would incur small expenses for the funeral and invest any money that they would have received from the insurance and the deceased's estate.

Life has no guarantees but it's important to care for our loved ones while they are still alive and never try to show a sign of appreciation when they have passed on.

Author's Personal Profile

Mr Letshego Tau was born on 22 April 1984. He grew up, attended and completed school in the small town called Wepener, and he holds numerous academic qualifications, including a bachelor's degree in public management from the Central University of Technology, South Africa in 2009, a national diploma in public management from the same university, a certificate in public procurement and supply management with seventy-two credits (NQF level 6); advance contract management SLAs and benchmarking certificate, a demand management certificate from PALAMA (Public Administration Leadership and Management Academy of South Africa), and a certificate in how to avoid fruitless, wasteful, unauthorised, and irregular expenditure in supply chain procurement.

His academic credentials prove that he has been a valuable asset in the South African government as an employee within the procurement field.

Mr Letshego Tau was vetted for security clearance while working for the Provincial Department of Health in the Free State by the National Intelligence Agency and was issued with a certificate valid for a period of five years from the date of 15 April 2010 to 30 April 2015.

Author's Work Experience

Mr Tau also worked for the Department of Treasury as an Intern within Supply Chain Management for a period of one year and was promoted to the Department of Health in the Free State as supply chain practitioner in the Demand Management Section within the Supply Chain Chief Directorate, where he worked for a period of three years and was promoted as a senior supply chain practitioner at Universitas Academic Hospital in the Supply Chain Management Unit. From January 2012, Mr Letshego Tau was appointed as acquisition and contract specialist for Centlec State Owned Company until he developed a love for writing.

His inspiration for writing came as a result of reading lots and lots of inspirational and business books.

Mr Tau's motto in life is '*In life, no sky is the limit, only you can limit yourself.*'